THE LYRICS
OF
SYD BARRETT

ISBN: 978-1-787-60256-4

Many thanks to Syd Barrett Music Ltd and Paul Loasby, Andy Murray
and Elena Bello at One Fifteen for their kind assistance.

All words written by Syd Barrett

'Birdie Hop', 'Bob Dylan Blues', 'Butterfly', 'Dolly Rocker', 'Double O Bo',
'Let's Split', 'Lucy Leave', 'Milky Way', 'Opal', 'Two Of A Kind' and 'Word
Song' (Barrett) published by Rock Music Company Ltd.

'Apples And Oranges', 'Astronomy Domine', 'Bike', 'Chapter 24',
'Flaming', 'The Gnome', 'Jugband Blues', 'Lucifer Sam', 'Matilda Mother',
'The Scarecrow', 'Scream Thy Last Scream', 'See Emily Play' and
'Vegetable Man' (Barrett) published by Westminster Music Ltd.

'Arnold Layne' and 'Candy And A Currant Bun' (Barrett)
published by Dunmo Music Publishing Ltd./
Peer Music Ltd./Syd Barrett Music Ltd.

'Baby Lemonade', 'Clowns And Jugglers', 'Dark Globe', 'Dominoes',
'Effervescing Elephant', 'Feel', 'Gigolo Aunt', 'Here I Go', 'I Never Lied To
You', 'If It's In You', 'It Is Obvious', 'Late Night', 'Long Gone', 'Love Song',
Love You', 'Maisie', 'No Good Trying', 'No Man's Land', 'Octopus', 'Rats',
'She Took A Long Cool Look', 'Swan Lee (Silas Lang)', 'Terrapin',
'Waving My Arms In The Air', 'Wined And Dined' and
'Wolfpack' (Barrett) published by Lupus Music Ltd.

Printed in Malta

A catalogue record for this book is available from the British Library.

www.omnibuspress.com

THE LYRICS
OF
SYD BARRETT

OMNIBUS PRESS

London / New York / Paris / Sydney / Copenhagen / Berlin / Madrid / Tokyo

Syd Barrett's lyrics were never officially printed in his lifetime and have never been annotated in an authorised form. We reproduce the most definitive version possible here, acknowledging the kind input of David Gilmour and Rob Chapman.

Contents

Syd, London,
1967.
[Michael Ochs
Archives/Getty]

Foreword

SYD BARRETT LOVED pop music, he loved painting, he loved women, he loved dope, he loved clothes and he loved writing and recording music.

When I first knew the Floyd they hardly did any original songs; they were a blues band who did weird solos instead of the virtuoso guitar solos of Eric Clapton, Peter Green etc. Similarly, Syd's singing had no virtuoso curliques – he was no Rod Stewart, Long John Baldry or Jack Bruce. His songwriting was not particularly stylish nor crammed with hits or grandiloquence, yet it was endlessly surprising and apparently effortless.

Syd's style of songwriting, playing and singing was the foundation of Pink Floyd, inspiring many bands to build great designs and to explore the new sounds and approaches that opened the door to electronic pop music. All of this set the path for the Floyd, who went on to become the most important UK band in the twentieth century, after the Beatles, through their influence on future music as well as in sales. Without the Floyd there may never have been hip-hop, concept albums, electronica or computer/ synthesiser-driven pop/dance music.

Syd, like most great writers, was a collector, whether borrowing James Joyce's 'Golden Hair' for a song, or a Love track for 'Interstellar Overdrive', or from Lewis Carroll or Edward Lear. Syd wrote songs about clothes, fetishism, astronomy, space travel and Eastern mysticism.

Before I knew Syd, he had already written many songs, a lot of them very 'childlike'. He seemed to have a strong connection to the innocence of childhood. Later, he could turn his descriptive abilities on himself through his confusion about life and his role in it. 'Scream Thy Last Scream', 'Vegetable Man' (written in my sitting room) and 'Jugband Blues' are the most gut-wrenching self-analyses that one could possibly imagine; Van Gogh's late paintings come to mind. A year or two earlier he was writing 'See Emily Play' or 'Bike', and a couple of years before that, 'Effervescing Elephant'.

Syd was handsome, he painted pictures, he had lovely girlfriends, he was an effortless leader of a revolutionary band. He disappeared into the fog and none of us could get him back. We all loved him and wished he was still with us, still writing those great songs and opening up new ways of thinking about music or playing inspired improvisation. He got multimedia before it had been invented; he would have been an incredible digital artist, as well as all the other things that he was.

When I pass Earlham Street, Seven Dials, The Roundhouse, Powis Square, Tottenham Court Road or Abbey Road, my mind flips back to Syd.

He changed my life, he changed our world, but did he ever get to enjoy it? Perhaps the very vision that he had turned inwards on himself rather than being passed on to us.

I hope he was happy in his later life, and I hope he decided that the music business was something he did not want to know about. I hope he knows we were all there ready to help him, but he seemed not to want us. We lost a friend and an inspiration, but his work lives on in his lyrics and his songs, and in all the people and artists he inspired, whether they knew it or not.

As the years go by, I am constantly reminded of the impact that Syd's work has had around the world. I once found myself in Moscow sat next to Tom Stoppard during a performance of *Rock 'n' Roll*. Stoppard's play takes place in Czechoslovakia in the late Sixties and revolves around the life of a young Czech musician. In conversation with Tom, I discovered that he based the musician on a 'Syd Barrett character', in a vastly different setting.

Syd's life and story led Tom Stoppard to engage with the challenges of being a creative person in a rapidly changing and often difficult world. It is an attribute to Syd, an important musician and artist of the Sixties in London, that his work inspires others across different media, times and places.

He was a brief but close friend. I miss him and his creativity.

I am proud to have worked with him through good times and confusing ones. Maybe Syd really is the 'Piper at the Gates of Dawn'.

He certainly opened up many minds.

Peter Jenner

*Pink Floyd at the Casa Madrona
Hotel, Sausalito, CA, November
1967. [Baron Wolman]*

Introduction

"You only have to read the lines of scribbly black and everything shines"

SYD BARRETT BEGAN and ended his creative life as a painter but, for an
all too brief period in the 1960s, he painted magnificently in sound and
in song. David Gilmour maintains that, had he persisted as a songwriter,
Syd's legacy would have been assured. "The guy was a real innovator. One
of the three or four greats, along with Dylan," he told Nick Kent of *NME* in
1973. All we listeners ever got was a tantalising glimpse of a creative spirit
that burned brightly but was all too rapidly extinguished. Syd left a slender
body of work, comprising three singles and two albums with Pink Floyd, a
couple of solo albums and a belatedly released LP of outtakes. Combined
with a clutch of songs that were never released in his lifetime and only saw
the light of day on Pink Floyd's *The Early Years 1965–1972* box set in 2011,
the sum total of all that creative effort and energy is the 52 published
songs gathered here. They are arranged alphabetically rather than in
the order they were recorded, but a pattern of development still reveals
itself. The collection begins with the nifty nimble wordplay of 'Apples And
Oranges' and the bittersweet tale of the transvestite 'Arnold Layne' , and
ends with the abstract fragments of 'Wolfpack' and 'Word Song', the former
a scatter gun fusillade of imagery, the latter a dispassionate compendium
of the vocabulary that had once made its writer so innovative and unique.
Words stripped of all context, just laid out end to end.

Although he enjoyed all the benefits of a secure middle-class
upbringing, Syd Barrett wasn't an intellectual or an academic high-flyer.
Apart from his beloved art classes, formal education was more of a
hindrance than a passion. He left school with three O levels, and only just
scraped by with the lowest pass grade in English Literature. His reading
habits followed as impulsive a path as he did and, apart from a few vague
references in interviews to the fairy tales he enjoyed as a child, he was
not, by his own admission, widely read. What he clearly had in abundance,
though, was a remarkable facility for wordplay.

Syd's gift was for the descriptive. Although it's a well-aired truism that
pop lyrics rarely work as well in print as they do when wedded to the beat,
it seems to me that many of the images and inscapes contained in Syd's
songs come alive just as capably on the flat canvas of the page. Because
he had such an intuitive grasp of the internal rhythm of words, the songs
retain their bounce, especially when read aloud. He adopted assonance
and internal rhyme to great effect, and made clever use of ellipses and

elision. The songs shimmer with painterly images: "Watching buttercups cup the light", "Pussy willow that smiled on this leaf", "A broken pier on the wavy sea", "When the rooftops shone dark". There's the exquisite applique of the sequinned fan in 'No Good Trying', the brandished wand "with a feathery tong" in 'Dark Globe'. Some songs readily lend themselves to cartoon frames or woodcut captions. Some read like they should be interwoven into a tapestry or frieze: "Gazing through trees in sorrow", "She'll be scrubbing bubbles on all fours", "I prowled in the evening sun's glaze", "Warm shallow waters sweep shells". Syd used idiosyncratic phraseology and quaintly old-fashioned terms that appear only rarely in Sixties pop and rock. "In love with you and your charms" in 'Lucy Leave', "She don't do the Stroll" in 'Here I Go', "Jiving on down" in 'Gigolo Aunt', "with her slinky look" in 'Waving My Arms In The Air'. Women are everywhere but there is an absence of machismo. There's always more about courtship than conquest. There's a "mean go-getter" in 'If It's In You' but it sounds tongue in cheek. Syd's lyrics frequently run counter to the idea of rock'n'roll swagger and often betray a lack of psychological armoury, mockingly in "Please, you know I'm feeling frail", and touchingly in "I don't care if I'm nervous with you", but with primal urgency and anguish in the more heartfelt of his solo recordings.

That's not to say that the songs always make sense. At times there is a wilful disregard for being understood; it's as if coherence is not part of the plan. Syd's lyrics, particularly on the solo albums, hint at meaning in fleeting bursts, but many of them are the product of a very irregular head that refuses to yield up its internal logic. It's a brave listener who would offer an interpretation of what's going on in 'Rats' or 'No Man's Land'. If Syd's songs were paintings, many of them would consist entirely of vanishing points and receding perspectives. All too often sense is grasped briefly but rapidly diminishes to an echo. As the man himself sang on 'Wolfpack', "the life that was ours/Grows sharper and stronger away and beyond". He may have first burst onto the scene with concise nursery-rhyme vignettes that distilled the very essence of that magical, mythical 1967 Summer of Love but, within a matter of months, he was adopting the free verse techniques of an early twentieth-century modernist.

LIKE MANY OF his generation, Syd Barrett started off learning guitar licks in the school common room and college canteen. He played in R&B covers bands and did what everyone does at that age: he copied his heroes until he found his own style. It was the same with his lyric writing. There is a hint of parodic blues vernacular ("Mean treating me and done me harm, Lucy") in one of his earliest recorded efforts, 'Lucy Leave'. The tendency still lingers as late as 1970 in 'Dolly Rocker' ("She done went out and paid for me"). 'Double O Bo', another of Pink Floyd's earliest recorded songs, was a gimmicky pastiche of Bo Diddley's self-referential songwriting and owes a considerable debt to the man's own 'Bo Diddley Is A Gunslinger'. 'Bob Dylan Blues', another early effort, alludes to several tracks from *The Freewheelin' Bob Dylan* album. "Look, it's the me and you from every town," Syd said to girlfriend Libby Gausden, as they saw the crowd arriving to see Dylan on his first British tour in 1964. 'Candy And A Currant Bun', the B-side to Pink Floyd's first single, 'Arnold Layne', borrowed its riff from Howlin' Wolf's 'Smokestack Lightnin'' and was originally called 'Let's Roll Another One' (sample lyric "I'm high/Don't try to spoil my fun"). Syd simply overhauled the song a couple of years later, dropped in a reference to his school tuck shop, and sneaked a cleverly disguised "fuck" into the first chorus (which made the song far more suggestive than it had been when it was simply about smoking pot).

Once he had developed a degree of expertise in his borrowings, Syd wrote some of his best songs. An instinctive flair for comic verse gave us 'Effervescing Elephant', a perfect Hilaire Belloc pastiche and probably the most metrically sophisticated song he ever wrote. The lyric is enunciated at a bracing lick, utilises panic and breathlessness to good effect, and is pitch perfect. At any one moment, an incorrectly calibrated word or phrase would cause the entire edifice to collapse like a pack of cards. Instead, momentum and mounting tension are sustained with a lightness of touch and little flourishes of genius: "Everyone was nervy" instead of nervous, "But all in vain" lifted directly from Belloc's 'Matilda' and that final dismissive "And you're all too scant" to make the concluding truncated rhyme. Syd's love of Belloc peaks with 'Matilda Mother', where the original lyric was adopted piecemeal from 'Jim', 'Henry King', and 'Matilda' from *Cautionary Tales For Children*. Even when forced by the Belloc estate to change the words, Syd borrowed one again, this time lifting the first line of his alternative lyric from the children's verse 'When Good King Arthur Ruled This Land'.

The other notable pastiche song that Syd wrote was 'Swan Lee'. Although it didn't appear on vinyl until the 1988 *Opel* LP, the song had been written long before he made *The Madcap Laughs* (1970) and was in fact the first he endeavoured to record as a solo artist. It's Syd's attempt to write in the style of Henry Longfellow's epic poem 'The Song Of Hiawatha'. He adheres loosely to Longfellow's trochee verse style (the same form appears in Cream's 'Tales Of Brave Ulysses' and had been much parodied by Lewis Carroll and others a century earlier).

With 'Octopus' Syd utilises an art school approach to found materials in his borrowings. In an interview with Giovanni Dadomo for *Sounds*, he cited 'Green Grow The Rushes Ho' as an inspiration, a remarkably un-rock'n'roll source for song material in the late 1960s. In the same interview, he mentions having books by Shakespeare and Chaucer just lying around at home and candidly admits, "I don't really read a lot. Maybe I should." 'Octopus' gives us a rare glimpse into Syd's experimental technique. It's the only song he ever talked about at length, evidently proud of the sheer amount of effort that appears to have gone into making it work. Originally called 'Clowns And Jugglers', the song takes its opening "trip to heave and ho" refrain from *Summer's Last Will And Testament* by Elizabethan playwright Thomas Nashe. Elsewhere Syd lifts from 'Huff The Talbot' and 'Our Cat Tib' from the Mother Goose rhymes, and Shakespeare's *Henry VI, Part 1*, which features a character called Talbot and where the words "dragon", "wings", "ghost" and "tower" appear in the first five pages. Other sources include John Clare's poem 'Fairy Things', Sir Henry Newbolt's 'Rilloby-Rill' and the anonymous children's rhyme 'Mr Nobody.' During the research for my Syd Barrett biography, *A Very Irregular Head*, I managed to locate the source material for many of these lines. They are to be found in *The Junior Laurel & Gold Anthology*, compiled by John R. Crossland and first published by Collins in 1936. By the time Syd was born in 1946, the book was in its seventh impression. All these skilfully utilised verse fragments are woven into the kaleidoscopic pattern of images and evocations without ever once breaking rhythm. Even when the meaning is elusive and the thought processes choppy and fragmented, the whole thing remains metrically consistent. It's easy to view 'Octopus' purely as a conceptual exercise – Syd applying his fine art training in found materials to pop lyric and sacrificing conventional narrative flow in the process – but it's equally easy to overlook the quality of his own phrase-making in that remarkable song. "The drones they throng on mossy seats" is worthy of a nineteenth-century lake poet. "Little minute gong/coughs and clears his throat" is another of Syd's exquisite cartoon miniatures, out of the same mould as "she'll be scrubbing bubbles on all fours". 'Clowns And Jugglers' and 'Octopus' reveal his genius for extrapolating and rearranging. It's tempting to ponder how many other times he did this in song without us knowing, where the phrases are so expertly lifted and sifted that we simply have no idea of their origins. It's a very precise craft. You only have to compare the original wording of the nineteenth-century circus poster that John Lennon found in a junk shop with the way he refashioned them in 'Being For The Benefit Of Mr Kite' to see how expertly the borrowing can be done. In 'Octopus', for example, Syd takes John Clare's original line "filled with little mystic shining seed" and changes it to "mystic shining feed". One simple change, but it makes all the difference without altering the meaning. It's easy to reduce all this to a dry scholastic exercise but that's not what's going on here. This is a man considering words carefully, a man who is used to sitting in front of a canvas and thinking very precisely about how and where to apply paint. There's nothing slapdash about it, as there is in some of Syd's less successfully realised songs. It's all carefully thought through.

A similar gift is evident in 'Chapter 24' from *The Piper At The Gates Of Dawn* LP. Set to one of Pink Floyd's most beautiful melodies, the lyric is borrowed from the Fu / Return Hexagram of the *I Ching*, which is linked with the month of the Solstice. The original version, in translation, runs as follows:

THE JUDGMENT
RETURN. Success.
Going out and coming in without error.
Friends come without blame.
To and fro goes the way.
On the seventh day comes return.
It furthers one to have somewhere to go.

ONE OF THE chief characteristics of Syd's very early lyrics is their easy conviviality and conversational tone. 'Bike', with its invitations and disclaimers, is full of the mannered conventions and polite gentility of refined table talk: "I'd give it to you if I could, but I borrowed it", "Take a couple if you wish, they're on the dish", "If you think it could look good, then I guess it should". When he's in a joyous mood, Syd's songs are peppered with exclamations; the exuberant "no fear", "yippee" and "hooray" that burst like fireworks all over *The Piper At The Gates Of Dawn*. The sudden yelled interjection of "Thought you might like to know" in 'Apples And Oranges', the cautionary "Oh my goodness" in 'Effervescing Elephant', the jubilant "whoopee" in 'Love You' and "hee hee" in 'Birdie Hop'. At times the tone darkens into the impeccably enunciated sarcasm of "It's awfully considerate of you" and "I'm most obliged to you" in 'Jugband Blues'. Later the conversational voice becomes more drawling and ragged – "It is obvious/May I say, oh baby, that it is found on another plane" – but the spoken rhythms remain intact. Elsewhere there's the colloquial "no fear" in 'Flaming', and the unmistakably East Anglian "seen you looking good the other evening" in 'Love You'. Certain songs have the rambling, ambling disposition of inconsequential chat. Others contain sudden digressions and asides. The exasperated "Oh understand" of 'No Man's Land', the paranoid undertow of "if you think you're unloved/Then we know about that" in 'Rats', the mocking and dismissive "A big band is far better than you" in 'Here I Go'. Even in the most convoluted of Syd's lyrics, familiar everyday speech patterns are never far away.

Songs about gnomes, bicycles, scarecrows and fairy tales have come to define Syd's image as the poster boy for psychedelia, but these whimsical idylls were penned in a relatively short period of time and comprise only a small proportion of his work. Syd's Cambridge friends remember his charm and geniality, but they also remember a caustic, satirical wit who did not suffer fools gladly. There is a bite to his lyrics from very early on that stands in sharp contrast to the flower-child innocence of 'Flaming' and 'Matilda Mother'. 'Arnold Layne' might at first be regarded as one of those typically 1967 songs about a dysfunctional spirit, out of the same mould as The Who's 'I'm A Boy' and 'Happy Jack', but Syd sneers "Now he's caught – a nasty sort of person" in the final verse and interjects a sense of condemnation into what, up until that point, had been up a quirky tale about one man's sexual peccadilloes. On the B-side to 'Arnold Layne', 'Candy And A Currant Bun', there's the small matter of that jealous and menacing middle eight – "Don't try another cat tonight/Don't go a lot on that" – which seems to hold the girl to account for his insecurity. 'Bob Dylan Blues' might be an affectionate pastiche, but it is also a warning about false prophets, commercialisation, slavish fan conformity, affected image and how clothes resolutely do not maketh the man. In this respect 'Bob Dylan Blues' is not as far removed in spirit from 'Vegetable Man' as might initially be assumed. The tone is more acerbic and self-loathing in the latter song, but the sentiments are similar: "It's what I wear, it's what you see/It must be me, it's what I am". Interpreted by some as a literal self-analysis of Syd's own deteriorating mental condition, it is equally a statement about the hollowness of persona and is delivered with audible bitterness and bile. Not too many other songwriters, caught up in the halcyon spirit of that flower power summer, were penning lines like "In my paisley shirt, I look a jerk", even if many of them clearly suited the sentiment.

The sardonic tone became more evident as Syd's disillusion with fame increased. By the time he wrote and recorded 'Jugband Blues' – the last Pink Floyd song credited in his name – on 19 October 1967, he had married impeccably mannered speech to impeccably delivered derision. The tone resurfaces in several of Syd's solo songs. 'Let's Split' contains just three short verses and runs for just over two minutes but it is riddled with irritability. The discontent of a man in retreat from commitment is conveyed in a barracking mantra of "hound, hound, hound/Back down, down, down". In 'Feel' he seems to be mocking the continued attentions of the women who were still lining up for his favours at that time: "How I love you to be by my side, they wail". There's a harassed and harrowing tone to these songs that isn't so apparent when Syd was singing about scarecrows and gnomes, but there's traces of it all along – even as early as 1965 with the disavowals and distancing in 'Lucy Leave'.

There are phrases and images contained in these pages that are utterly unique to Syd's idiosyncratic vernacular. No one else could have written these songs. No one else wrote pop lyrics that sound remotely like them: "Life to this love to me – heading me down to me", "Flaking you are, a

...yd with sister
...osemary at the
...aside, 1949;
...Bournemouth,
...967; with
...isky the cat
...his garden,
...lls Road,
...mbridge,
...963.
...yd Barrett
...usic Ltd]

Tortoise *by Syd
Barrett, 1963.
[Syd Barrett
Music Ltd]*

nice little one/To put it all around, it's just good/I like it", "I lay as if in surround", "The end of truth that lay out the time", "Dimples dangerous and blessed", "Magnesium, proverbs and sobs". Such wordplay springs from a very unorthodox sensibility and answers to its own grammatical rules. Prepositions, verbs, transitives and indefinite articles frequently don't function as they should. An oddly positioned phrase either makes you marvel at his gifts or puzzle as to why coherence and sense were jettisoned so wilfully. Why "the earth streams in, in the morning" rather than 'light'? Why "Life that comes of no harm" rather than 'to no harm'? Why "He isn't love on Sunday's Mail" rather than 'in' and "Did I winking of this" rather than 'at this' in 'If It's In You'? Why she "gazed all over my arm" rather than 'on over' in 'She Took A Long Cool Look'? Clarity, precision and the purposeful leap out of almost every song, but so too do the oblique and the unintelligible.

When Syd was at his creative peak, the lyrics could be conveyed in the sheer dazzling be-bop dexterity of "Got a flip-top pack of cigarettes in her pocket/Feeling good at the top/Shopping at shops" or with utter simplicity in the three short verses of 'See Emily Play'. He often expressed himself in truncated couplets – "Rain falls in grey far away", "She held a torch on the porch", "The land in silence stands", "I stood very still by the window sill" – but when he was in the fog, when friends noticed he no longer had a sunny disposition, the lyrics began to convey a sense of unravelling. Even then, though, a purposeful phrase, with clear measured articulation, hints at faculties that are only slowly being surrendered. Witness the way the cavalcade of wordplay stumbles and fumbles and dolly drifts its way through 'It Is Obvious', before culminating in imagery that conveys the expressive gifts of a natural versifier: "And the trees by the waving corn stranded/My legs move the last empty inches to you/The softness the warmth and the weather in suspense".

Assonance was often deployed for the sheer love of sound – "Floating down, the sound resounds/Around the icy waters underground", "Padding around on the ground/He'll be found when you're around" – sometimes those simpatico vowel sounds are aligned to the lazy elisions of slow-motion momentum: "Fangs all round the clam/Is dark below the boulders hiding all/The sunlight's good for us". Syd frequently used ellipses and elision in this way to convey or sabotage meaning. Those truncations and jump cuts were there from very early on. 'Arnold Layne', with its "Moonshine, washing line" and "Doors bang, chain gang", put such devices in the pop charts. At times you can sense where the three bracketed dots of an ellipsis should go; at others you can't see the join. There are unexpected shifts in perspective. Phrases seem to fold in on themselves and linearity is abandoned. There are sudden mergers of incongruities. Sometimes these convergences convey the linguistic traits of someone experiencing synaesthesia: the "clouds of sunlight" in 'Matilda Mother', "Alone in the clouds all blue" in 'Flaming', "light misted fog" in 'Wolfpack'. At other times – "Come around, make it soon, so alone", "Away far too empty, oh so alone" – heartfelt sentiments fragment into a telegrammed shorthand of despair.

SYD'S DESCRIPTIVE POWERS often pivot on stasis and momentum. There is the stillness of Emily "Gazing through trees in sorrow", the stillness of a wheat field scarecrow and Syd very still by the window sill in 'Late Night'. Elsewhere images of agitated propulsion proliferate: the old woman who flings her arms madly; the flails and gasps; the chugging and strolling and cornering neatly and striding out to meet 'Maisie' in the evening light; the spinning around and around in a car; the shoulder pressing in the hall; the rocking horse in 'No Good Trying' and "the other room" full of chiming, chinging automata in 'Bike' just waiting to be activated. Because it is set to a slowed down music-hall lilt, the conclusion of 'Bike', disarms the listener, but it's an astounding shift in perception after all that talk of gingerbread men and mice called Gerald – a portal verse where Syd can be glimpsed slipping through a tear in the space-time continuum in order to orchestrate a whole other world of mechanical activity in that room of musical tunes. The Syd who can do that is a shapeshifter, a conjurer. Later a palpable sadness settles on the songs. They remain wistful at times, but you get the impression that the clocks don't chime and bells don't ring anymore. After a while they were increasingly about stasis, Syd inhabiting the scarecrow whose "head did no thinking/His arms didn't move". The lyrics begin to betray the Syd who just wanted to merge with the light show and no longer did very much onstage.

Behind the façade though, there was a febrile imagination still frantically whirring away. "He was rotating inside. Inside he was a dynamo of energy," said poet Spike Hawkins, who knew Syd in the late Sixties. It's a perfect description of the Syd who would no longer play the showbiz game. The pop star was turning into a refusenik, but the songs remained full of kinetic impulse. The dreamlike immersion of 'Astronomy Domine' turns into the slow-mo "A-move about is all we do" of 'Terrapin'. The Siam cat pads and prowls in 'Lucifer Sam'. Syd adopts a sinister prowl in 'Long Gone'. There's the quicksand immobilisation of "My legs move the last empty inches to you", the petulance of "I got up and I stomped around", the mysterious animation of "If I mention your name/Turn around on a chain". There's the bird who hops, the prowling tiger, the straggling crab, the sheer restless compulsion of "Hey ho, never be still". There's a fair amount of plummeting too. "I like the fall that brings me to", "My head kissed the ground/I was half the way down", "We awful awful crawl", "Senses in the gravel", "heading me down to me", "So high you go, so low you creep".

At times there is a sense of suspended animation: "Why d'ya have to leave me there/Hanging in my infant air"; "Please leave us here/Close our eyes to the Octopus rise". The words of 'Wolfpack', with its images of wheeling and hovering, seem to swirl and tumble in accord with the melody. When it works, when momentum is married to that unique sensibility and things don't stray into incoherence, it is wondrous. 'Love You' and 'Gigolo Aunt' (which share similar chord progressions) both bound along "at a madcap galloping chase". In 'Rats', the crazed impetus pushes sense to the very edge of meaning, culminating in the maniacal cavalcade of "Cable, gable, splintra, channel/Top the seam he's taken off".

SYD'S SONGS OFTEN present a sense of the unknowable. The narrative flow seems arbitrary and inexplicable. The lyrics frequently lack specifics. They trigger multiple associations in the mind and suggest myriad meanings which they do not ultimately reveal. Sometimes it's as if he's only filled in half of the canvas and wandered off mid-song. What's going on at the beginning of 'Baby Lemonade'? I always imagine a taciturn drinker cradling a pint and looking out of a pub window at a crowd of wintertime carousers or car park pissheads. You probably get a different image. Things are rarely made explicit. In 'Dominoes', who do you imagine playing the game? A boy with an elderly uncle or aunt? Two people in a pub? Two lovers? Syd's songs are full of vague approximations and riddling compressions of thought. "Don't you want to see her prove?" Prove what? "If it's there will you go there too?" Where is there and what is it? "I give you half" in 'Rats'; "Half and half" in 'Waving My Arms In The Air'. Half of what? Syd's songs are frequently puzzles with several key pieces missing. At times you feel like you are listening to the Syd who teased and taunted his fellow band members in one of their final recording sessions with a song called 'Have You Got It Yet?', where the chorus response required them to sing "no no no", and where Syd kept changing it every time. There are moments when 'Have You Got It Yet?' sounds like the most appropriate song he could have written.

Syd's use of elisions and ellipsis sometimes erase sense altogether. There are songs in which no one line seems to follow the logic of the previous one. This fragmentary perspective is often presented as a facet of Syd's mental disintegration. Rather than psychoanalyse irregular metre as a manifestation of his gradual decline, I believe that he was pursuing a form of abstraction in his writing, utilising methods that would have been second nature to him as a painter, and indeed to many of the twentieth century's most accomplished exponents of free verse. In the same way that modernist novelists and poets were finding new ways to blur boundaries between the figurative and the non-figurative, I think Syd was trying to do something similar in his songs. He said as much in a stoned, rambling interview in the summer of 1967 with the American journalist Meatball Fulton, where he expressed a desire to apply some of his art school teachings to his music and songwriting.

When Syd and Spike Hawkins hung out, they often played with Hawkins' Poetry Broth, a cut-up game of words and phrases. There are few detectable cut-ups in Syd's songwriting – "Colonel with gloves Strauss leeches" in 'If It's In You' and the word jumbles of 'Rats' and 'Word Song' being the only obvious ones – but the technique was clearly incorporated into his working methodology. The experiments don't always succeed. In some of the later songs there's a lack of application, and he betrays an inability or unwillingness to tidy. That gift for precision grows undisciplined and unruly. The beautiful melody and opening lines of 'Birdie Hop' descend into lazy word (dis)association. 'Dolly Rocker' and 'Milky Way' seem to fall apart too. But that's the nature of experimentation: sometimes you fail. I'm sure some people won't buy this theory and will regard these songs as acid addled nonsense – the product of a man who is simply in the process of losing his marbles – but then the same people would have said that at the time about 'Strawberry Fields Forever' or 'I Am The Walrus'. They would have said it about the English poetry underground and the experimental stanzas of Pete Brown, Spike Hawkins and Bob Cobbing. They would have said it about improvised music, modern jazz, tape loops, multimedia happenings and abstract art, the world that Syd was immersed in and emerged from and, in the case of modern jazz, eventually retreated back to in his latter-day listening habits. A child of five could do that, the detractors would say of a Picasso or a Jackson Pollock. To which the only reasoned response is "yes, but could you?"

Syd Barrett only had to read the lines of scribbly black and everything shined. He peered into the doll's house darkness and evoked worlds based on what he saw there. He made the marionettes dance and the woodland creatures pause in their tracks. Sometimes the songs were crystalline, dayglo or neon lit, at other times they were murky and muddied, opaque and illogical. His palette was messy but bursting with colour. The words splattered out onto the page. Here they all are. Flicker, flicker, flicker, blam, pow!

Rob Chapman

(Overleaf)
Rehearsing
for 'See Emily
Play' on Top
of the Pops, 6
July 1967. [LFI/
Photoshot]

Artworks by
Syd Barrett.
Clockwise from
top) Autumn
Berries and
Leaves, 1963;
Little Red
Rooster, 1964;
Self Portrait,
circa 1961.
[Syd Barrett
Music Ltd]

The Lyrics
of Syd Barrett

Apples And Oranges

Got a flip-top pack of cigarettes in her pocket
Feeling good at the top
Shopping at shops
She's walking in the sunshine town
Feeling very cool
At the butchers and the bakers and the supermarket stores
Getting everything she wants from the supermarket stores
Apples and oranges
Apples and oranges

Cornering neatly she trips up sweetly
To meet the people
She's on time again
And then
I catch her by the eye
Then I stop and have to think
What a funny thing to do 'cos I'm feeling very pink
Apples and oranges
Apples and oranges

I love she
She loves me
See you, see you, see you

Apples and oranges

Thought you might like to know
I'm her lorry driver man
She's on her own
Down by the river side
Feeding ducks in the afternoon tide (quack quack)
Apples and oranges
Apples and oranges
Apples and oranges

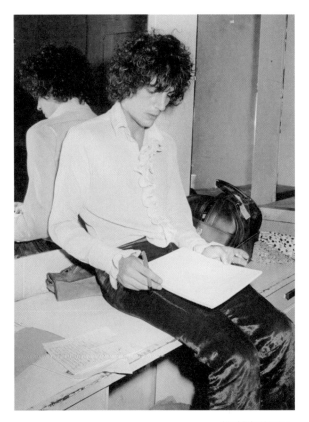

In a club dressing room,
London, 1967.
[Koh Hasebe/Shinko
Music/Getty]

Arnold Layne

Arnold Layne had a strange hobby
Collecting clothes
Moonshine, washing line
They suit him fine
On the wall hung a tall mirror
Distorted view, see through baby blue
He dug it

Oh, Arnold Layne
It's not the same
Takes two to know
Two to know, two to know, two to know
Why can't you see?
Arnold Layne, Arnold Layne, Arnold Layne, Arnold Layne

Now he's caught – a nasty sort of person
They gave him time
Doors bang, chain gang
He hate it

Oh, Arnold Layne
It's not the same
Takes two to know
Two to know, two to know
Why can't you see?
Arnold Layne, Arnold Layne
Arnold Layne don't do it again

ink Floyd before
their gig at the
olden Circle,
tockholm,
eptember 1967.
ars Groth/TT
ews Agency/
A Images]

Astronomy Domine

Lime and limpet green, a second scene
A fight between the blue you once knew
Floating down, the sound resounds
Around the icy waters underground
Jupiter and Saturn, Oberon, Miranda and Titania
Neptune, Titan, stars can frighten

Blinding signs flap
Flicker, flicker, flicker blam, pow, pow
Stairway scared, Dan Dare who's there?

Lime and limpet green
The sound surrounds the icy waters under...
Lime and limpet green
The sound surrounds the icy waters underground

Baby Lemonade

In the sad town
Cold iron hands
Clap the party of clowns outside
Rain falls in grey far away
Please, please, Baby Lemonade

In the evening, sun going down
When the earth streams in, in the morning
Send a cage through the post
Make your name like a ghost
Please, please, Baby Lemonade

I'm screaming, I met you this way
You were nice to me like ice
In the clock they sent through a washing machine
Come around, make it soon, so alone
Please, please, Baby Lemonade

In the sad town
Cold iron hands
Clap the party of clowns outside
Rain falls in grey far away
Please, please, Baby Lemonade

In the evening, sun going down
When the earth streams in, in the morning
Send a cage through the post
Make your name like a ghost
Please, please, Baby Lemonade

Bike

I've got a bike, you can ride it if you like
It's got a basket, a bell that rings and things to make it look good
I'd give it to you if I could, but I borrowed it

You're the kind of girl that fits in with my world
I'll give you anything, everything if you want things

I've got a cloak, it's a bit of a joke
There's a tear up the front, it's red and black, I've had it for months
If you think it could look good, then I guess it should

You're the kind of girl that fits in with my world
I'll give you anything, everything if you want things

I know a mouse, and he hasn't got a house
I don't know why I call him Gerald
He's getting rather old, but he's a good mouse

You're the kind of girl that fits in with my world
I'll give you anything, everything if you want things

I've got a clan of gingerbread men
Here are men, there are men, lots of gingerbread men
Take a couple if you wish, they're on the dish

You're the kind of girl that fits in with my world
I'll give you anything, everything if you want things

I know a room of musical tunes
Some rhyme, some ching, most of them are clockwork
Let's go into the other room and make them work

Birdie Hop

Birdie Hop – he do, he hop along
A lonely bird upon a window there
Hee hee, there he blow
A windy snow, he knew the snow
I know the snow, a hoppy bird

The antelope ride around the parasol
Just to see if he's a man
Enough to meet you in the sandpit
On a flying kind of sighing in a meddlesome bay
You know the way – I see the flies
She's a little kite, the sort you think
You might like to fire
And like a kite you get to see her every night
You know the way
She's only paving her way
Ektachrome plane – I see the flies

Birdie Hop – he do, he hop along
A lonely bird upon a window there
Hee hee, there he blow
The windy snow, he know the snow
A hoppy bird

A camel woke up to a Polish dawn
Wouldn't look to see his feet had gone
He wouldn't like it
Wouldn't have the strength to fight it
I see the flies
I'm the only bird, a little third
I lost a quarter
Had a yearning to be earning just a dollar a day
And in a way you shouldn't like it, Ektachrome plane
I see the flies

Bob Dylan Blues

Got the Bob Dylan blues
And the Bob Dylan shoes
And my clothes and my hair's in a mess
But you know I just couldn't care less

Gonna write me a song
'Bout what's right and what's wrong
'Bout God and my girl and all that
Quiet while I make like a cat

'Cos I'm a poet, don't ya know it
And the wind, you can blow it
'Cos I'm Mr. Dylan, the king
And I'm free as a bird on the wing

Roam from town to town
Guess I get people down
But I don't care too much about that
'Cos my gut and my wallet are fat

Make a whole lotta dough
But I deserve it though
I've got soul and a good heart of gold
So I'll sing about war and the cold

'Cos I'm a poet, don't ya know it
And the wind, you can blow it
'Cos I'm Mr. Dylan, the king
And I'm free as a bird on the wing

Well I sings about dreams
And I rhymes it with seems
'Cos it seems that my dream always means
That I can prophesy all kinds of things

Well the guy that digs me
Should try hard to see
That he buys all my discs in a hat
And when I'm in town go see that

'Cos I'm a poet, don't ya know it
And the wind, you can blow it
'Cos I'm Mr. Dylan, the king
And I'm free as a bird on the wing

Butterfly

Listen all you girlies even though I haven't met you
Gonna catch you soon in my butterfly net
You better watch out

Some time when I watch you
I stretch out my hand to touch you
'Cos it drives me wild
To see you flutter by
You butterfly

I won't squeeze you dead
Pin things through your head
I just want your love

I won't write your name
In Latin in a frame
'Cos framing is a shame

Listen all you girlies even though I haven't met you
Gonna catch you soon in my butterfly net
You better watch out

Candy And A Currant Bun

Oh my, girl sitting in the sun
Go buy, candy and a currant bun
I like to see you
Lick that

Oooh, don't talk to me
Please, just walk with me
Please, you know I'm feeling frail

It's true, sun shining very bright
It's you, I'm gonna love tonight
Ice cream, taste good in the afternoon
Ice cream, taste good if you eat it soon

Oooh, don't touch me child
Please, you know you drive me wild
Please, you know I'm feeling frail

Don't try another cat tonight
Don't go a lot on that
You must know
I'm very very very frail

Oh my, girl sitting in the sun
Go buy, candy and a currant bun
I like to see you run
In flight

Pink Floyd, EMI publicity
shoot, London, 1967.
[Dezo Hoffman/
Shutterstock]

Chapter 24

All movement is accomplished in six stages
And the seventh brings return
For seven is the number of the young light
It forms when darkness is increased by one
Change return success
Going and coming without error
Action brings good fortune
Sunset

The time is with the month of winter solstice
When the change is due to come
Thunder in the Earth, the course of heaven
Things cannot be destroyed once and for all
Change return success
Going and coming without error
Action brings good fortune
Sunset, sunrise

All movement is accomplished in six stages
And the seventh brings return
For seven is the number of the young light
It forms when darkness is increased by one
Change return success
Going and coming without error
Action brings good fortune
Sunset, sunrise

Clowns And Jugglers

Trip to heave and ho, up down, to and fro
You have no word
Trip, trip to a dream dragon
Hide your wings in a ghost tower
Sails cackling at every plate we break
Was cracked by scattered needles
The little minute gong
Coughs and clears his throat
Madam you see before you stand
Hey ho, never be still
The old original favourite grand
Grasshoppers green Herbarian band
And the tune they play is in us confide
So trip to heave and ho, up down, to and fro
You have no word
Please leave us here
Close our eyes to the Octopus ride

Isn't it good to be lost in the wood
Isn't it bad so quiet there, in the wood
Meant even less to me than I thought
With a honey plough of yellow prickly seeds
Clover honey pots and mystic shining feed

The madcap laughed at the man on the border
Hey ho, Huff the Talbot
The winds they blew and the leaves should wag
And they'll never put me in their bag
The raging seas will always seep
So high you go, so low you creep
The wind it blows in tropical heat
The drones they throng on mossy seats
The squeaking door will always squeak
Two up, two down we'll never meet
Please leave us here
Close our eyes to the Octopus ride
Please leave us here
Close our eyes to the Octopus ride

Dark Globe

Oh where are you now
Pussy willow that smiled on this leaf?
When I was alone you promised a stone from your heart
My head kissed the ground
I was half the way down, treading the sand
Please, please, lift a hand
I'm only a person whose armbands beads
On his hands, hang tall
Won't you miss me?
Wouldn't you miss me at all?

The poppy bird's way
Swing twigs coffee brands around
Brandish a wand with a feathery tong
My head kissed the ground
I was half the way down, treading the sand
Please, please, please lift a hand
I'm only a person with Eskimo chain
I tattooed my brain all the way
Won't you miss me?
Wouldn't you miss me at all?

Dolly Rocker

I know a sweet girl
She done went out and paid for me
Done a sweet girl
After five we went for tea
She seen a Dolly Rocker
She want a girl, she got her
I wanna see her, I know I do
I love you darling, all for you

You want to meet Pearl?
She's as cute as a squirrel's nut
She done seen me
Said she thought she got the lot
She's a Dolly Rocker
Want to wait 'till I got her
Said she know I know we know I do
Said she gotta see me lonely with you

Oceans may travel, away so long
Senses in the gravel, to see yourself at home
Nice to be at home
All there'll ever be forever
All my life, you see, when you got her
All I know, you know, I show you, baby
Through your head push to you, baby
Is a Dolly Rocker
She know what she got her
She seen a Dolly Rocker
She seen a Dolly Rocker

Dominoes

It's an idea, someday
In my tears, my dreams
Don't you want to see her prove?
Life that comes of no harm
You and I, you and I and dominoes
The day goes by

You and I in place
Wasting time on dominoes
A day so dark, so warm
Life that comes of no harm
You and I and dominoes
Time goes by

Fireworks and heat, someday
Gold a shell, a stick or play
Overheard a lark today
Losing when my mind's astray
Don't you want to know with your pretty hair
Stretch out your hand, glad fields
In an echo for your way

It's an idea, someday
In my tears, my dreams
Don't you want to see her prove?
Life that comes of no harm
You and I and dominoes
The day goes by

Double O Bo

Bo Diddley was a private eye
Hand was fast and his IQ high
Dealer say "Double O, you won't last
Slow down boy, you're livin' too fast"

Well, Double O had a Cadillac
Machine guns and a bullet-proof back
Engine taken from a 707
Sounds like a sure way of getting to heaven

Anyone put 5 pounds of lead
To keep Bo Diddley from getting dead
Nothing he had won't keep him alive
Was a snub-nosed pistol, a Colt 45

Well, Bo drank gallons of rye and bourbon
Martinis dry and you better serve them
Martinis so dry, the shaker burst
Bo keeled on his side and died of thirst

Pink Floyd on the steps
of EMI House, London,
4 March 1967.
[AP/Shutterstock]

Effervescing Elephant

An effervescing elephant
With tiny eyes and great big trunk
Once whispered to the tiny ear
The ear of one inferior
That by next June he'd die, oh yeah
Because the tiger would roam
The little one said: "Oh my goodness I must stay at home

And every time I hear a growl
I'll know the tiger's on the prowl
And I'll be really safe, you know
The elephant he told me so"
Everyone was nervy, oh yeah
And the message was spread
To zebra, mongoose, and the dirty hippopotamus

Who wallowed in the mud and chewed
His spicy hippo-plankton food
And tended to ignore the word
Preferring to survey a herd
Of stupid water bison, oh yeah
And all the jungle took fright
And ran around for all the day and the night

But all in vain, because, you see
The tiger came and said: "Who me?
You know, I wouldn't hurt not one of you
I'd much prefer something to chew
And you're all too scant." Oh yeah
He ate the elephant

Feel

You feel me
Away far too empty, oh so alone
I want to come home
Oh find me inside of a nocturne – the blonde
How I love you to be by my side they wail
The crab on her side
She straggled a bridge by the water

She misses her craw
Folly grew
Heady aside in a dell
Inside and I be the lonely one, my bride
How I leave on the waddling wheel they flail
A gasp shringing, a bad bell's ringing
The angel, the daughter

You feel me
Away far too empty, oh so alone
I want to come home
Oh find me inside of a nocturne – the blonde
How I love you to be by my side they wail
The crab on her side
She straggled a bridge by the water

Flaming

Alone in the clouds all blue
Lying on an eiderdown
Yippee, you can't see me
But I can you

Lazing in the foggy dew
Sitting on a unicorn
No fear, you can't hear me
But I can you

Watching buttercups cup the light
Sleeping on a dandelion
Too much, I won't touch you
But then I might

Screaming through the starlit sky
Travelling by telephone
Hey ho, here we go
Ever so high

Alone in the clouds all blue
Lying on an eiderdown
Yippee, you can't see me
But I can you

Gigolo Aunt

Grooving around in a trench coat
With the satin on trail
Seems to be all around in tin and lead pail, we pale
Jiving on down to the beach
To see the blue and the grey
Seems to be all on, it's rosy, it's a beautiful day

Will you please keep on the track
'Cos I almost want you back
'Cos I know what you are
You are a gigolo aunt, you're the gigolo aunt
Yes I know what you are
You are a gigolo aunt, you're a gigolo aunt

Heading on down with the light, the dust in your way
She was angrier there, than her watershell male
Life to this love to me – heading me down to me
Thunderbird shale
Seems to be all on, it's rosy, it's a beautiful day

Will you please keep on the track
'Cos I almost want you back
'Cos I know what you are
You are a gigolo aunt, you're a gigolo aunt
Yes I know what you are
You are a gigolo aunt, you're a gigolo aunt

Grooving on down in a knapsack superlative day
Some wish she move and just as she came move jiving away
She made the scene should have been, superlative day
Everything's all on, it's rosy, it's a beautiful day

Will you please keep on the track
'Cos I almost want you back
'Cos I know what you are
You are a gigolo aunt, you're a gigolo aunt
Yes I know what you are
You are a gigolo aunt, you're a gigolo aunt

*Pink Floyd, Blackhill
Enterprises publicity
shoot, 1966. [Marc
Sharrett/Shutterstock]*

The Gnome

I want to tell you a story
About a little man
If I can
A gnome named Grimble Gromble
And little gnomes stay in their homes
Eating, sleeping, drinking their wine

He wore a scarlet tunic
A blue green hood
It looked quite good
He had a big adventure
Amidst the grass
Fresh air at last
Wining, dining, biding his time

And then one day – hooray!
Another way for gnomes to say
Hooray

Look at the sky, look at the river
Isn't it good?
Look at the sky, look at the river
Isn't it good?
Winding, finding places to go

And then one day – hooray!
Another way for gnomes to say
Hooray
Hooray

Here I Go

This here's a story about a girl that I knew
She didn't like my songs
And that made me feel blue
She said: "A big band is far better than you"

She don't rock'n'roll, she don't like it
She don't do the Stroll, well she don't do it right
Well, everything's wrong and my patience was gone
When I woke one morning
And remembered this song
Oh-oh-oh, kinda catchy
I hoped that she would talk to me now
And even allow me to hold her hand
And forget that old band

I strolled around to her pad
Her light was off and that's bad
Her sister said that my girl was gone
"But come inside, boy, and play, play, play me a song"
I said "Yeah! Here I go"
She's kinda cute don't you know
That after a while of seeing her smile
I knew we could make it, make it in style

So now I've got all I need
She and I are in love, we've agreed
She likes this song and my others too
So now you see my world is

Because of this tune
What a boon this tune
I tell you soon
We'll be lying in bed, happily wed
And I won't think of that girl
Or what she said

I Never Lied To You

There will be shoulder pressing in the hall
And I won't know if you're here at all

There will be wine and drinking in the yard
There won't be anybody very hard
There will be lots of things that we can do

And all and more will be for you
Everything I knew I tried with you
But everything to you was never easy
So I went ahead around my world
I saw the things you do arriving by your side
To see you looking too
But I know this I know
I never lied to you
It's been just like you're gone
For just one day for so long
It's been so hard to bear with you not there
But though I think of you
The things you do when I'm with you
To be with you, to be alone
Can only be why I am here
What's meant to be

If It's In You

Yes I'm thinking of this, yes I am
Puddletown Tom was the underground
Hold you tighter so close, yes you are
Please hold on to the steel rail

Colonel with gloves Strauss leeches
He isn't love on Sunday's Mail
All the fives crock Henrietta
She's a mean go-getter
Got to write her a letter

Did I winking of this, I am
Yum yummy yam doh, yummy yam youm yom
Yes, I'm thinking of this, in steam
Skeleton kiss to the steel rail

Fleas in Pamela gloves Strauss leeches
Chugging along with a funnel of steam
All the fives crock Henrietta
She's a mean go-getter
Got to write her a letter

It Is Obvious

It is obvious
May I say, oh baby, that it is found on another plane
Yes I can creep into cupboards, sleep in the hall
Your stars, my stars, are simple cot bars
Only an impulse, pie in the sky
Mumble listen dolly
Drift over your mind – holly
Creep into bed when your head's on the ground
She held a torch on the porch
And she winked an eye

The reason it is written on the brambles
Stranded on the spikes – my blood red, oh listen
Remember those times I could call
Through the clear daytime and you'd be there

Braver and braver, a handkerchief waver
The louder your lips to a loud hailer
Growing to gather, the good of each other
The wandering, stumbling, fumbling, rumbling
Minds shot together
Our minds shot together

So equally over a valley, a hill wood
And quarry stood, each of us crying
A velvet curtain of grey
Mark the blanket where sparrows play
And the trees by the waving corn stranded
My legs move the last empty inches to you
The softness, the warmth and the weather in suspense
Mog to a grog, the star of white chalk
Minds shot together, our minds shot together

Jugband Blues

It's awfully considerate of you to think of me here
And I'm most obliged to you for making it clear
That I'm not here
And I never knew the moon could be so big
And I never knew the moon could be so blue
And I'm grateful that you threw away my old shoes
And brought me here instead dressed in red
And I'm wondering who could be writing this song

I don't care if the sun don't shine
And I don't care if nothing is mine
And I don't care if I'm nervous with you
I'll do my loving in the winter

And the sea isn't green
And I love the Queen
And what exactly is a dream
And what exactly is a joke

*The only photo shoot to
include both Syd Barrett
and David Gilmour,
January 1968. [Peter
Jenner/Pink Floyd Archive]*

Late Night

When I woke up today
And you weren't there to play
Then I wanted to be with you
When you showed me your eyes
Whispered love at the skies
Then I wanted to stay with you

Inside me I feel alone and unreal
And the way you kiss will always be
A very special thing to me

When I lay still at night
Seeing stars high and light
Then I wanted to be with you
When the rooftops shone dark
All alone saw a spark
Spark of love just to stay with you

Inside me I feel alone and unreal
And the way you kiss will always be
A very special thing to me

If I mention your name
Turn around on a chain
Then the sky opens up for you
When we grew very tall
When I saw you so small
Then I wanted to stay with you

Inside me I feel alone and unreal
And the way you kiss will always be
A very special thing to me

Let's Split

Everything about
About to go out
Me out, you out
Yes and everything is out
About, out
Out, out, out, out, out, out
Let's split
I'm telling you this is it

Everything is down
In hound, hound, hound
Back down, down, down
Even everything is down
Abound in down
Down, down, down, down, down
Let's split
Telling you this is it

Nobody is right tonight
Night, height, night, tight
It isn't right
Me out, you out
And everything is out
Out, out, out, out, out, out
Let's split

Long Gone

She was long gone, long, long gone
She was gone, gone, the bigger they come
The larger her hand 'till no one understands
Why for so long she'd been gone

And I stood very still by the window sill
And I wondered for those I love still
I cried in my mind where I stand behind
The beauty of love's in her eyes

She was long gone, long, long gone
She was gone, gone, the bigger they come
The larger her hand 'till no one understands
Why for so long she'd been gone

And I borrowed a page
From a leopard's cage
And I prowled in the evening sun's glaze
Her head lifted high to the light in the sky
The opening dawn on her face

She was long gone, long, long gone
She was gone, gone, the bigger they come
The larger her hand 'till no one understands
Why for so long she'd been gone

And I stood very still by the window sill
And I wondered for those I love still
I cried in my mind where I stand behind
The beauty of love's in her eyes

She was long gone, long, long gone

Love Song

I knew a girl and I like her still
She said she knew she would trust me
And I her will
I said: "OK baby, tell me what you be
And I'll lay my head down and see what I see"
By the time she was back
By her open eyes
I knew that I was in for a big surprise

I knew a girl and I like her still
She said she knew she would trust me
And I her will
I said: "OK baby, tell me what you be
And I'll lay my head down and see what I see"
By the time she was back
By her open eyes
I knew that I was in for a bigger surprise

Love You

Honey love you, honey little
Honey funny sunny morning
Love you more funny love in the skyline baby
Ice-cream 'scuse me
I seen you looking good the other evening

Oh, you dig it, had to smile just an hour or so
Are we in love like I think we be?
It ain't a long rhyme
It took ages to think
I think I'll hurl it in the water, baby

Honey love you, honey little
Honey funny sunny morning
Love you more funny love in the skyline baby
Ice-cream 'scuse me
I seen you looking good the other evening

Flaking you are, a nice little one
To put it all around, it's just good
I like it, hey hey hey
S'pose some time that day
Whoopee! Swing it along over across to me

Honey love you, honey little
Honey funny sunny morning
Love you more funny love in the skyline baby
Ice-cream 'scuse me
I seen you looking good the other evening

Goodtime rocker woman we'll stray our pieces
Little creepy we shine so sleepy
So whoopee!
That's how you look

Honey love you, honey little
Honey funny sunny morning
Love you more funny love in the skyline baby
Ice-cream 'scuse me
I seen you looking good the other evening

Adjusting a rubber duck
during rehearsals for
Games for May *at the*
Queen Elizabeth Hall,
London, 12 May 1967.
[Nick Hale/Hulton
Archive/Getty]

Lucifer Sam

Lucifer Sam, Siam cat
Always sitting by your side
Always by your side
That cat's something I can't explain

Jennifer Gentle you're a witch
You're the left side
He's the right side
Oh, no
That cat's something I can't explain

Lucifer go to sea
Be a hip cat, be a ship's cat
Somewhere, anywhere
That cat's something I can't explain

At night prowling sifting sand
Padding around on the ground
He'll be found when you're around
That cat's something I can't explain

Lucy Leave

Leave when I ask you to leave, Lucy
Please fall away from me, Lucy
Oh, go little girl
See that I'm so broken up about you, Lucy
Mean treating me and done me harm, Lucy
Being in love with you and your charms, Lucy
Oh, go little girl
I'm in love with you, Lucy
You got my heart, you got my heart, oh no
You tear me apart, you just won't let me go
You hold on so tight, so tight I just can't breathe
Now Lucy leave, Lucy

Leave when I ask you to leave, little girl
Please fall away from me, little girl
Yeah, go little girl
See that I'm so broke up about you, Lucy
Yeah, go

Maisie

Maisie, Maisie, Maisie, Maisie
Maisie
Bad luck
Bride of a bull
Strode out to meet Maisie in the evening light
Maisie
His luminous grin put her in a spin

Maisie, lay in the hall
With diamonds and emeralds
Maisie, Maisie
Bad luck
The bride of a bull strode out
To meet Maisie in the evening light
His luminous grin put her in a spin

Maisie lay in the hall with her emeralds
And diamond brooch, beyond reproach
Bad luck
Bride of a bull
Strode out
To meet Maisie in the evening light
Maisie

*Pink Floyd, EMI publicity
shoot, London, 1967.
[Dezo Hoffman/
Shutterstock]*

Matilda Mother

There was a king who ruled the land
His majesty was in command
With silver eyes the scarlet eagle
Showers silver on the people
Oh Mother, tell me more

Why d'ya have to leave me there
Hanging in my infant air waiting?
You only have to read the lines
Of scribbly black and everything shines

Across the stream with wooden shoes
Bells to tell the King the news
A thousand misty riders climb up
Higher once upon a time

Wondering and dreaming
The words have different meaning
Yes they did

For all the time spent in that room
The doll's house, darkness, old perfume
And fairy stories held me high
On clouds of sunlight floating by
Oh Mother, tell me more
Tell me more

Milky Way

What'd you ever say today
When you're in the milky way?
Oh tell me please
Just to give you a squeeze
If I met you – I told you what to do
Seems a while
Since I could smile the way you do

How many times, if I try, if I may
When you're in the milky way
Half of your time beside me only atmosphere
The singular, raised by heats and wet
Seems a while
Since I could smile the way you do

What can anyone mean to you
Standing in the milky way?

Take life easy
I mean so easy
Why so empty?
I told you, I can tell you
What to do when I hold you
And I tell you "I love you"
I feel that I'm... way you do

Give a gasp of life today
When you're in the milky way
Oh, try to please
Knock on wood of the trees
Glad you, mould you, mould you and hold you
Means five miles
And every way for you

*Practising
yoga at home,
29 Wetherby
Mansions, Earl's
Court Square,
London, 1969
[Aubrey Powell/
Hipgnosis]*

No Good Trying

It's no good trying to place your hand
Where I can't see because I understand
That you're different from me
Yes I can tell
That you can't be what you pretend
And you're rocking me backwards
And you're rocking towards
The red and yellow mane of a stallion horse

It's no good trying to hold your love
Where I can't see because I understand
That you're different from me
Yes I can tell
That you can't be what you pretend
The caterpillar hood won't cover the head
And you know you should be home in bed

It's no good holding your sequinned fan
Where I can't see because I understand
That you're different from me
Yes I can tell
That you can't be what you pretend
Yes you're spinning around and around in a car
With electric lights flashing very fast

No Man's Land

You would hold your head up high
You even try
You would hold another hand
Oh understand
They even see me under call
We under all
We awful awful crawl
To hear my ire
Come see me cry

Just searching you even try
I can make you smile
If it's there will you go there too?
When I live I die
They even see me under call
We under all, we awful awful crawl
Because of you, to see me be

Tell me, tell me, tell me, you need – need me so well
Shut your shop, shut your shop, listen, listen,
the horizon glows like a dove and I see
From a mild, shiny ocean, choke and weave in a spinning wheel
Pick up and tell love to me, open your door
Musty sugar with dust making stale it crows the near day
The cockerel, listen, listen, short choose of play,
Freedom of emotions and cracking my spleen 'cos we be us
Is wishing - pick up and tell love to me – open your door

Find – all I wish is shiver and whine the mean
could no notice to be as they be
Give a lot – listen listen – the grave sings you her song –
heavily spaced
All the crockery, china, war and spreading a spinning wheel
Opening, what a roll but you open the door, some time, long ago
Stream cool shallow water – seen a lot, seen a lot

Octopus

Trip to heave and ho, up down, to and fro
You have no word
Trip, trip to a dream dragon
Hide your wings in a ghost tower
Sails cackling at every plate we break

Was cracked by scattered needles
The little minute gong
Coughs and clears his throat
Madam you see before you stand
Hey ho, never be still
The old original favourite grand
Grasshoppers green Herbarian band
And the tune they play is in us confide

So trip to heave and ho, up down, to and fro
You have no word
Please leave us here
Close our eyes to the Octopus ride

Isn't it good to be lost in the wood
Isn't it bad so quiet there, in the wood
It meant even less to me than I thought
With a honey plough of yellow prickly seeds
Clover honey pots and mystic shining feed

Well, the madcap laughed at the man on the border
Hey ho, Huff the Talbot
Cheat, he cried shouting kangaroo
So true in their tree, they cried
Please leave us here
Close our eyes to the Octopus ride

Please leave us here
Close our eyes to the Octopus ride

Well, the madcap* laughed at the man on the border
Hey ho, Huff the Talbot
The winds they blew and the leaves did wag

They'll never put me in their bag
The seas will reach and always seep
So high you go, so low you creep
The wind it blows in tropical heat
The drones they throng on mossy seats
The squeaking door will always squeak
Two up, two down we'll never meet

So merrily trip and go my side
Please leave us here
Close our eyes to the Octopus ride

*Also 'mad cat'. David Gilmour's examination of the isolated vocal tracks reveals that Syd sings
'madcap' three times and 'mad cat' three times.

On stage at Olympia,
London, December
1967. [Ray Stevenson/
Shutterstock]

Opal*

On a distant shore, miles from land
Stands the ebony totem in ebony sand
A dream in a mist of grey
On a far distant shore

The pebble that stood alone
And driftwood lies half buried
Warm shallow waters sweep shells
So the cockles shine

A bare winding carcass, stark
Shimmers as flies scoop up meat, an empty way
Dry tears

Crisp flax squeaks tall reeds
Make a circle of grey in a summer way, around man
Stood on ground

I'm trying
I'm trying to find you
To find you
I'm living, I'm giving
To find you, to find you
I'm living, I'm living
I'm trying, I'm giving

*The original tape box and LP mistakenly listed this song as 'Opel'.

Rats

Gotta head down
Spot knock inside a spider
Said: That's love yeah, yeah, yeah, yeah
That's love yeah, yeah, yeah, yeah
Says: That's love – all know it
TV, teeth, feet, peace, feel it
That's love yeah, yeah, yeah, yeah
That's love yeah, yeah, yeah, yeah

Like the fall that brings me to
I like the fall that brings me to
I like the cord around sinew
I make a cord around sinew

Duck, the way to least is less
The deep craving of the metal west
Hell tomorrow's rain and test
Hell tomorrow's rain and test
Love an empty sun and guess
Love an empty sun and guess
Dimples dangerous and blessed

Heaving and arriving, tinkling
Mingling jets and statuettes
Seething wet we meeting fleck
Seething wet we meeting fleck
Lines and winds and fib and half
Of each fair day I give you half
Of each fair day I give you half
I look into your eyes and you
Flake in the sun for you

Bam, spastic, tactile engine
Heaving, crackle, slinky, dormy, roofy, wham
I'll have them, fried bloke
Broken jardy, cardy, smoocho, mucho, paki, pufftle
Sploshette moxy, very smelly
Cable, gable, splintra, channel
Top the seam he's taken off

Rats, rats lay down flat
We don't need you, we act like that
And if you think you're unloved
Then we know about that
Rats, rats, lay down flat
Yes, yes, yes, yes, lay down flat

The Scarecrow

The black and green scarecrow as everyone knows
Stood with a bird on his hat and straw everywhere
He didn't care
He stood in a field where barley grows

His head did no thinking
His arms didn't move except when the wind cut up rough
And mice ran around on the ground
He stood in a field where barley grows

The black and green scarecrow was sadder than me
But now he's resigned to his fate
'Cos life's not unkind – he doesn't mind
He stood in a field where barley grows

On keyboards
recording for
A Saucerful of
Secrets, De La
Lea Studios,
London, October
1967. [Andrew
Whittuck/
Redferns/Getty]

Pink Floyd, January 1967.
[Tony Gale/Pictorial Press]

Scream Thy Last Scream

Scream thy last scream old woman with a casket
Blam blam your pointers point your pointers
Waddle with apples to grouchy Mrs Stores
She'll be scrubbing bubbles on all fours

Scream thy last scream old woman with a casket
Fling your arms madly old lady with a daughter
Flat tops of houses, mouses, houses
Fittle and tittle are sitting fat fat

Watching the telly 'till all hours, telly time
Fling your arms madly old lady with a daughter

Scream thy last scream old woman with a casket
Blam blam your pointers point your pointers
Waddle with apples to grouchy Mrs Stores
She'll be scrubbing bubbles on all fours

Scream thy last scream old woman with a casket

See Emily Play

Emily tries but misunderstands
She's often inclined to borrow somebody's dreams till tomorrow
There is no other day
Let's try it another way
You'll lose your mind and play
Free games for May
See Emily play

Soon after dark Emily cries
Gazing through trees in sorrow hardly a sound till tomorrow
There is no other day
Let's try it another way
You'll lose your mind and play
Free games for May
See Emily play

Put on a gown that touches the ground
Float on a river forever and ever, Emily, Emily
There is no other day
Let's try it another way
You'll lose your mind and play
Free games for May
See Emily play

*On stage with Richard
Wright at the* International
Times *Free Speech
Benefit, London,
29 April 1967.*
[Michael Putland/Getty]

She Took A Long Cool Look

She took a long cool look at me
And smiled and gazed all over my arm
She loves to see me get down to ground
She hasn't time just to be with me

A face between all she means to be
To be extreme, just to be extreme
A broken pier on the wavy sea
She wonders why all she wants to see
But I got up and I stomped around
And hit the piece where the trees touch the ground

The end of truth that lay out the time
Spent lazing here on a painting green
A mile or more in a foreign clime
To see farther inside of me

And looking high up into the sky
I breathe as the water streams over me

Swan Lee (Silas Lang)

Swan Lee got up at the Running Foot pow-wow
And padded from the fire to his waiting canoe
Chattering Squaw untied the wigwam door
The chief blew smoke rings two by two

The land in silence stands

Swan Lee, his boat by the bank in the darkness
Loosened the rope in the creepers entwined
A feather from the wing of a wild young eagle
Pointed to the land where his fortune he'd find

The land in silence stands

Swan Lee paddled on from the land of his fathers
His eyes scanned the undergrowth on either side
From the shore hung a hot, heavy, creature-infested tropic
Swan Lee had a bow by his side

The land in silence stands

Swan Lee crept home, half on land, half on water
Grizzly bear and raccoon his fare
He followed his ears to the great waterfall
Swan Lee knew people and his squaw was there

The land in silence stands

Suddenly the rush of the mighty great thunder
Confronted Swan Lee as this song he sang
In the dawn, with his squaw, he was paddling homewards
It was all written down by Long Silas Lang

The land in silence stands
The land in silence stands
The land in silence stands

Terrapin

I really love you and I mean you
The star above you, crystal blue
Well, oh baby, my hair's on end about you

I wouldn't see you and I love to
I fly above you, yes I do
Well, oh baby, my hair's on end about you

Floating, bumping, noses dodge a tooth
The fins are luminous
Fangs all round the clam
Is dark below the boulders hiding all
The sunlight's good for us
'Cos we're the fishes and all we do
A-move about is all we do
Well, oh baby, my hair's on end about you

Floating, bumping, noses dodge a tooth
The fins are luminous
Fangs all round the clam
Is dark below the boulders hiding all
The sunlight's good for us
'Cos we're the fishes and all we do
A-move about is all we do
Well, oh baby, my hair's on end about you

I really love you and I mean you
The star above you, crystal blue
Well, oh baby, my hair's on end about you

Two Of A Kind

Open your eyes and don't be blind
Can't you see we're two of a kind?
I've got to say this, I hope you don't mind
I love you, we're two of a kind

Just ask yourself and you will find
We go together, we're two of a kind
No use protesting, be resigned
Baby you know, we're two of a kind

I knew it when I saw you
I felt it a little more when
I talked with you at first
All my blues dispersed
I couldn't disguise
My complete surprise
When you were feeling it too
I'm in love with you, I'm in love with you

Open your eyes and don't be blind
Can't you see we're two of a kind?
I've got to say this, I hope you don't mind
I love you, we're two of a kind

Backstage at the Saville Theatre, London, 1 October 1967. [GAB Archive/Redferns/Getty]

Vegetable Man

In yellow shoes I get the blues
So I walk the streets with my plastic feet
With blue velvet trousers make me feel pink
There's a kind of stink about blue velvet trousers
In my paisley shirt, I look a jerk
And my turquoise waistcoat is quite outta sight
But oh, oh, my haircut looks so bad

Vegetable man
Where are you?

So I change my gear, and I bind my knees
And I cover them up with the latest cut
And my pants and socks are bought in a box
It doesn't take long to find nylon socks
The watch, black watch, my watch
With a black face and a date in a little hole
And all the luck, it's what I got
It's what I wear, it's what you see
It must be me, it's what I am

Vegetable man
Where are you?

I've been looking all over the place for a place for me
But it ain't anywhere
It just ain't anywhere
Vegetable man, vegetable man, vegetable man
Vegetable man, vegetable man, vegetable man
He's the kind of fella you just gotta see if you can
Vegetable man

Waving My Arms In The Air

Waving my arms in the air
Love my love, got no care
No care, no, no
Pressing my feet to the ground
Stand up right where you stand
Call to you and what do you do
Laying back in a chair

She's so high on the air
She's so high on the air
Half and half, half and half
All you have to do to call
Is hold her hand, stand a while
And a smile and we'll understand
Yes we do – yes, yes we do

Oh, what a girl I got too
Oh, what a girl I got too
With her slinky look she held her tie to her hair
And I could see everywhere
No-one in the land, no-one
No-one in the land, no-one
But it rains on Saturday
Cats and dogs in the hay
Stormy day, hey, hey
And you shouldn't try to be
What you can't be
And you shouldn't try to be
What you can't be
Call to you and what do you do

Wined And Dined

Wined and dined, oh it seemed just like a dream
Girl was so kind
Kind of love I'd never seen
Only last summer, it's not so long ago
Just last summer, now musk winds blow

Wined and dined, oh it seemed just like a dream
Girl was so kind
Kind of love I'd never seen

Wined and dined, oh it seemed just like a dream
Girl was so kind
Kind of love I'd never seen

Chalk underfoot, life I should prove
Dancing in heat, our love and you

Wined and dined, oh it seemed just like a dream
Girl was so kind
Kind of love I'd never seen

Wolfpack

Howling, the pack in formation appears
Diamonds and clubs, light misted fog, the dead
Waving us back in formation
The pack in formation

Bowling they bat as a group
And the leader is seen – so early
The pack on their backs, the fighters
Through misty the waving – the pack in formation
Far reaching waves
On sight, shone right
I lay as if in surround

All enmeshing, hovering
The milder I gaze
All the animals laying trail
Beyond the far winds
Mild the reflecting electricity eyes
Tears, the life that was ours
Grows sharper and stronger away and beyond
Short wheeling – fresh spring
Gripped with blanched bones, moaned
Magnesium, proverbs and sobs

Howling, the pack in formation appears
Diamonds and clubs, light misted fog, the dead
Waving us back in formation
The pack in formation

Word Song

Stained, glaucous, glycerine, gold, goat, plover
Gold, local, stocks, type, food, wild, national, lake, flag
Valve, gyroscope, sect
Heat, helium, leg, fair, state, invention, medieval
Refraction, faction, alter, action
Hunter, interest, bullock, market

Loads, liquids, neon, eaters, jaws, jungle
Main, signal, knives, kitchen
Ingot, lovey, mirror, mould
Myacene, moat, poppy, rubber
Radar, rags, sugar, teak
Silver, pug, tin, beetroot
Carrot, ebony, fruit, copper, silk

Car, distant, pigmy, hid, pack
Timber, pudding, straw
Raindrops, pattering, ramps
Chameleon, prairie, pods, trigger
Museum, scales, square, ultra, pot of, map, vent
Volcano, vain, wreck, tactic
Tidal, arches, valley, hand
Inflect, impression, loom, last, molten
You, gamma, meeting
Lighting, signal, Ireland, coral, cold

Aboard a ferry en route to
the Star Club, Copenhagen,
Denmark, September 1967.
[Pink Floyd Music Ltd]